KELLETT'S CHRISTMAS

A Hundred
Christmas Poems

by

Arnold Kellett

with illustrations by
Philip Spence

To our grandchildren

*Benjamin, Rachel, Molly, Sam, Jessie,
Martha, Hannah, Dan, Lily, Chloe,
Max, Rosie, Jake and Thomas*

© Arnold Kellett 1998

Published by Foundery Press

ISBN 1 85852 115 7

INTRODUCTION

This is an updated and greatly-extended version of the anthology published in 1988 by Foundery Press, which the publishers called *Kellett's Christmas*. I have decided to keep the title, partly because it is nicely alliterative, and partly because what follows does indeed represent my view of Christmas.

Before you read any of it, though, I would like to clear up possible misunderstandings. First, please don't imagine that I ever sat down to write a book consisting of a hundred poems on Christmas! It is simply that over a period of about forty years it has been my custom to celebrate each Christmas by writing a poem or two – and this is the resulting total. Many appeared in print for the first time in the *Methodist Recorder,* others in magazines such as *The Dalesman,* and many have been read at Christmas services and entertainments all over the country and abroad.

But how on earth could one person write a hundred poems all on the same topic? Well, I find the subject inexhaustible. Christmas is such a complex and colourful amalgam of history, theology and folklore, and has evolved into such a vast, international beanfeast, with all kinds of sociological and commercial overtones. There is always something new to be said about it, no end of changes to be rung on the old Christmas bells.

In these poems I have generally used rhyme rather than blank or free verse, because this, I think, is what most people prefer. Above all, I have aimed at being understood. The problem with so much modern verse is that it is too difficult and obscure, sometimes deliberately so, as though poets, by muddying the water, can make it seem deeper. Where there is anything that needs explanation or commentary I have added notes, including those at the back on Christmas origins.

Another possible misunderstanding arises from the fact that many of these could be seen as protest poems . . . I *love* Christmas! With all its faults and failings I still enter into it with an unbounded enthusiasm undiminished by the passing years. In particular, I love the romantic atmosphere that can be generated by the surviving mid-winter customs of our pre-Christian forefathers – the Celtic mistletoe, the Roman Saturnalia, the Yule-tide of the Anglo-Saxons and Vikings. I also treasure our little family customs, such as still setting up the Nativity scene I made for our first child – on top of the TV set, to show what should have priority!

Even so, the mainspring of much of this verse is a sense of the *scandal* of Christmas, which I consider to be two-fold. First, the way so many manage to celebrate the birth of Christ without giving him a serious thought. The sour-faced old Puritan in one of my poems, so scandalised by this reversion to paganism that he tried to abolish Christmas, went to ridiculous extremes. The art of keeping Christmas is to get the balance right between pagan mid-winter revelry and the spiritual rejoicing which comes from an understanding of who Jesus was.

As I see it, when Jesus was born it was as though the Author of the whole human drama, long hidden behind the scenes, had stepped out on to the stage of history. Jesus is, according to the New Testament, 'the image of the invisible God', the one who came to bring us fullness of life, both in this world and in the next. *This* is what we are supposed to be celebrating! It is nothing less than the Eternal Word becoming flesh and blood, living amongst us.

Secondly, there is the scandal of those who celebrate the birth of Jesus – of all people – by extravagant self-indulgence. What irony is here! Have we forgotten that Mary said in her pre-natal meditation: 'He has filled the hungry with good things, and the rich he has sent empty away'? The Puritans were wrong. There's every reason to eat, drink and be merry at Christmas. But to do this in the name of Christ, and at the same time remain indifferent to the needs of the poor, the hungry, the sick and the suffering, is a mockery. True, there is often at Christmas a remarkable, if short-lived, outpouring of compassion and generosity. Yet we do well to ask ourselves: what have we given to those in need *compared with what we spend on ourselves, our families and friends?*

So this is another theme – the crying need for money to be given to worthy causes. Previous sales of these poems have raised considerable sums for the Save the Children Fund and for land-mine victims. All author's royalties from this edition will go to The Methodist Relief and Development Fund. What the author hopes, however, is not only to raise money but to encourage continuing support for this and other relief organisations – all inspired by some new insight into the meaning of the coming of Christ.

Happy Christmas!

Arnold Kellett
Knaresborough
North Yorkshire

2

FOREWORD

It is good news that Dr Arnold Kellett has produced this further collection of his poems around the Christmas themes. His combinations of fun and earnestness, of enjoying Christmas and lamenting its trivialities, of sensing both the profundity and the profligacy, make for reflection both delightful and deep. Thank you, Arnold.

It is a sign of the genuineness of these reflections that he has devoted the royalties to the Methodist Relief and Development Fund, of which I was Chairman until recently. The MRDF rejoices at such welcome generosity, for it desperately needs all the gifts and encouragement it can get in a society that is somewhat bored now by the everlasting demands of the world's poor. They do not go away. Funds like ours are stretched to the limit and we are always having to turn people away.

Two features of MRDF work resonate well with Christmas themes. First, we help out in emergency relief situations where there are instant victims of flood or famine, war or pestilence, but try too to direct much of our energy to the long-term. We like to help those who are devising schemes to improve things for years ahead, and to make people self-sufficient. It hardly needs to be pointed out that the Christmas truth is for the long-term of humankind, not just aid to the people of Judaea in the first century. Second, we have a special eye for the small-scale, the almost insignificant whom nobody else bothers about – some wells here, a chicken farm started there, a special school set up in a village here and a hospice in a township there, miles away from the media and the notice of the great public. Christmas has that feel too. A tiny baby born into a backwater of empire is the central symbol. Small is both beautiful and altogether significant.

So please enjoy all these poems to the full; may Christmas be both plain good fun and full of hope for all the world.

Richard G. Jones

MILLENNIUM

Millennium! Why make such a fuss?
What's it got to do with us?
Why! Two thousand years, you see,
Since Christ was born to start AD.

No! That's not true – the Gospels say
That Christ was born in Herod's day,
And since historians all agree
That Herod died in 4 BC,
The Bethlehem birth, we can be sure,
Is chronologically premature.

Our calendars are quirkish things,
Rearranged by popes and kings . . .
Two thousand years, then, let's retrace
To when the birth of Christ took place . . .
The Millennium we would have to fix
In Nineteen Hundred and Ninety-Six!

We've missed the Millennium! It's passed us by!
(Some with great relief would sigh!)
But does it matter? Dates are rough,
And history's made of stronger stuff.

The Millennium can so rightly serve
A unique Christmas to observe,
And as the worldwide Church acclaims
The Name above all other names,
Countless billions turn to see
The turning-point of history:
Two thousand global years gone by –
Dated from a baby's cry.

CHRISTINGLE

(Written for children holding up cards at Christingle services, each saying a sentence of the acrostic – an explanation of the orange with candle and red ribbon.)

Christ for the world, the orange shows,
His the one true light;
Red the ribbon of his blood,
In love he bought our right:
Sins shall now be all forgiven
Through Good Friday's sacrifice,
Interfusing earth with heaven,
News of peace and paradise!
Goodness crowns our Christmas feast,
Lovely fruits of all the earth . . .
Every grateful Christian heart now celebrates
      the Saviour's birth.

ADVENT

The first candle lit!
The first tiny doors
Of Advent Calendars
Tweezed open by eager young fingers . . .
Christmas is coming!
Hark! the glad sound
Of whispered enquiries,
Of rustling paper,
The mounting tension
Of excited children
Probing and questioning
Their exhausted mothers . . .
How frenzied our work,
Swept on by the sense
Of growing momentum . . .

6

Was Robert Louis Stevenson right?
Better to travel hopefully
Than to arrive?
Is the pleasure all here
In anticipation,
In imagination,
In our expectation
Of how good it will be?

Advent is preparing . . .
Not shopping-days only,
Not spending on stomachs,
But clearing the mind,
And opening the heart
In readiness for something deeper
Than social fun and family reunion:
All may travel hopefully,
But only those who go as far as Bethlehem
Shall find arrival better than journey.

CHRISTMAS RUSH

Come to Church, the poster taunts,
Avoid the Christmas rush!
How true that worship comes in spurts:
The season strangely now converts,
And all without a blush
Will crowd the darkened door
For Midnight Eucharist or Mass;
A curious, unaccustomed sight,
So rarely are they here!
Far better worship week by week,
And all year round our Christmas keep –
Yet churches full of cheer
Eclipse the pagan feast . . .
So come and carol-in this Night,
Glad that priorities, for once, are right.

COMMERCIAL CHRISTMAS

Commercial Christmas! Hurry, hurry!
Get the sales in quick this year:
Easter eggs in January shops
Announce that summer's drawing near:
Far too early? Oh, come off it!
Early birds catch juicy profit.

Cut-throat competition clamours,
Sets the pace and calls the tune,
Scorns the seasons, bludgeons custom,
Selling Christmas cards in June;
And Santa's never in the red
Two jumps and half a year ahead!

Ever earlier Christmas pushes,
Forceful, false and out of place;
Come, ye money-spinning punters,
Join the annual reindeer-race!
And fix your thoughts, quite unperplexed,
Not on *this* Christmas – but the next!

IF JESUS HAD NEVER BEEN BORN

If Jesus had never been born,
There'd still be a Christmas by some other name:
We'd brighten mid-winter, and feast, just the same,
With corpulent turkey, and puddings and pies
And all the brave glitter that art can devise;
With satisfied stomach and contented mind
We'd purr with the pleasures of pagan mankind;
With greetings and gifts round the evergreen tree,
Like the jolly old Romans did, ages BC.

But we'd have no bright carols, no pealing of bells,
No tidings that Christ now in Bethlehem dwells,
No babe in the manger, no ox in the stall,
No angels, no shepherds, no good will to all;
No Mary, no Joseph, no Wise Men who came
To worship a King of unparalleled fame;
No Gospel to cheer us, no news to refresh,
No glad proclamation of God become flesh.

Then let us keep Christmas, the birth of the Boy
Who floodlights our darkness with infinite joy,
For God is now with us, to seek and to save,
To die for our sins and to rise from the grave,
To help us, to heal us, to bring us to bliss . . .
Yet, poorer than pagans, if, blind to all this,
We grope through our winter, depressed and forlorn . . .
Just as if Jesus had never been born.

A NICE THOUGHT

This Christmas I really must give
A substantial amount to a charity;
Just look at the way that they live –
Poor devils, what shocking disparity!
What a scandalous gulf now exists
Between millions near starving to death
And well-padded people like me –

Oh, talking's a sheer waste of breath:
Action's what counts! Where's my cheque-book?
And where did I put that address?
A hundredth of my Christmas spending
Could save some poor child in distress:
Now, I'm busy today – all this shopping –
I'll post off a nice cheque tomorrow . . .

But he doesn't . . . nor next day . . . nor ever,
For he's too busy drowning his sorrow
In good Christmas wining and dining,
As he feasts like a man worth his salt:
Good intentions, once more, pave the high road to Hell
And another child dies . . . by default.

SECOND COMING

Advent, if you know your Prayer Book,
Isn't just the gradual build-up
To the merry days of Christmas,
But a solemn, sharp reminder
Of the awesome Day of Judgment;
Christ shall come again in glory,
Reign supreme as King triumphant –
End of time, and end of story!

So, beyond our preparations,
Materialistic, earth-bound things,
Let us glimpse the lowly Christ-child
High enthroned as King of Kings,
Judge of every idle word,
All our weak, uncaring ways . . .
Then we'll see that Advent isn't
Ticking off the shopping days,
But thawing out our frozen hearts,
Sweeping clean a worthy place
For the new-born Prince of Peace,
Resplendent with his saving grace:
And Judgment Day we shall not dread,
Gathered round his manger bed.

EARTH LANDING

Man has walked the Moon;
Man shall soon tread Mars;
Man may circumnavigate
The far refulgent stars.

Cosmonauts shall soar
To probe the fringe of space . . .
But who will visit little Earth,
To cheer our wretched race?

Amidst the myriad suns,
Who cares for this poor speck
Of hate, and fear and loneliness?
Poor sub-atomic wreck!

Take heart! The very stars
Once blazed a Saviour's birth
And God so loved he mocked at space,
When Jesus walked the Earth!

CHRISTMAS BED

When you lie
Tucked up in bed
This Christmas Eve,
Just reflect
That Jesus said:
The Son of Man
Hath not where
To lay his head . . .
Born in straw,
He died on wood;
No bed for him:
Our glorious gain
Derives from bleeding
Saviourhood,
Our Christmas joy
Bought by his pain.

CHRISTMAS CARDS

How curious is the Christmas card;
Victorian invention
To celebrate the birth of Christ,
Who scarcely gets a mention.

But see these sentimental scenes
With bogus Yule-logs glowing,
And solemn robins wondering why
For them it's always snowing.

So once again, perennial chore,
We'll post our printed greeting,
And tick the everlasting list,
Mechanically repeating.

Until we reach a name we love,
Through death, alas, deleted –
Or one who sent no card last year
And made us feel quite cheated!

For friendships are reciprocal;
We must be systematic:
They sent a card, we'll send one back –
It's neat and democratic.

And cards for folk we never see
Are sent with no misgiving:
Just once a year, a signed receipt
To show that we're still living!

You're right, old Scrooge, there's humbug here!
But, still, it's not too tragic:
We'll shuffle multi-coloured cards,
Entranced by Christmas magic!

THE YEAR OF OUR LORD

A laser-beam in Bethlehem
Once burnt all time in two;
Before or after Christ we date
Every kingly potentate
From Rome to Timbuktu;
And every fact of history
Is registered in years BC,
Or privileged to qualify
For status Anno Domini;
And even atheists agree
To mark the time in strict AD,
And give to God his due.

O Light of civilising love,
Uniquely once you burned!
Yet still the gods of Mars and Thor
Ordain each brutalising war –
How little we have learned!
And how much better we should be
Than those who lived in mere BC!
Then let's wage war on sin and shame,
And justify our Christian name!
Thy Kingdom come! We'll work and pray;
The Year of Our Lord shall dawn today –
A title truly earned.

DIES NATALIS SOLIS INVICTI

The Day of the Birth of the Unconquered Sun

The Twenty-Fifth day of December –
A date so good to remember,
So firmly fixed in every mind,
To question it would seem unkind:
Yet if we take a careful look
Within the proper Christmas Book,
We find the Gospel writers state
No month or day of *any* date,
And we, in fact, have borrowed this
From pagan Roman revelries,
From Saturnalia's highest jinks,
For when the sun its lowest sinks,
And winter's solstice has begun,
They bring to birth the dying sun,
The Twenty-Fifth, the joyous feast,
For well-fed man and fattened beast,
For topsy-turvy drunken revels,
With Bacchus, Mithras, gods and devils,
A Roman carnival – no more,
And of one thing I am quite sure:
Though this – or any date – will do
To give to Christ the glory due,
Unless we work our utmost will . . .
The Twenty-Fifth is pagan still.

BETHLEHEM BONANZA

We're cashing in on Christmas!
We'll make a million quid!
For Jesus is big business
And let's not – God forbid!
Be slow to lavish Christmas cheer,
That's what the feast is for –
So join the Jesus jamboree
In swarming shop and store;
And spend with self-indulgent zeal –
For nothing is too dear;
Ye idle rich, be busy now –
It's only once a year!
The poor and hungry millions?
Ah, yes. That *is* a shame;
I wish that we could help them,
I wonder who's to blame . . .
But business here is booming:
Just think how much we'll take!
A Bethlehem bonanza!
And all for Jesus' sake!
Say, Mary! Joseph! Aren't you proud
To see the profits soar? . . .
But far away in Bethlehem
They'd shut the stable door.

THIRD WORLD CHRISTMAS

Christmas Eve, and all is well;
The presents wrapped, the food prepared;
The cosy room is bright with cards:
It's nice to know so many cared.

The children, warmly tucked in bed,
Have found a late, excited sleep,
And bulging sock and pillow-case
Await their first ecstatic peep.

Gathered round the glowing hearth
We lie relaxed and take our ease:
How calm and prosperous the time,
With no one but ourselves to please!

Let's put the television on . . .
Dear God! Some conscience-jabbing slum,
Where folk sit huddled in their rags,
With faces drawn and senses numb.

Where children stare with pleading eyes,
Where filth and fly-blown squalor dwell,
Where some, this night, will starve to death
Christmas Eve – and all is hell!

Then let us honour Mary's Child,
And comprehend why Jesus came . . .
To feed the hungry, heal the sick,
And cleanse our hearts with tears of shame.

LAST POST

No Christmas card this year from someone I care for;
No wonder I'm asking the why and the wherefore:
A Christmas card signature hastily penned
Can keep in repair the bond with a friend;
How much we rely on this annual link –
Mass-printed messages, endorsed in ink!

When was the last time I properly wrote
More than the minimal Christmas card note?
Or when did I visit – or talk on the phone?
What shameful neglect – and how time has flown!
Is it coolness – or illness? Could someone have died?
Is it lost in the post, submerged in the tide –
The Christmas-tide oceans of millions of cards
With their curt, unread tokens of seasonal regards?

No more! I shall make one New Year resolution:
Through a personal visit I'll seek absolution –
What's that? It's the card – last post, Christmas Eve!
The sense of relief I can hardly believe:
Relief just to see that familiar scrawl –
And to know that I shan't have to visit at all!

CHRISTMAS MORNING

Christmas morning! Sheer delight!
Father Christmas in the night
Lavished toys, and books, and sweets,
All the long-awaited treats!
Soon there'll be luxurious meals,
Bells will sound their rapturous peals,
Children sing the Saviour's birth,
Love, and joy, and peace on earth!

Christmas morning! Sheer distress!
Aching, hungry hopelessness:
In the night the fist of war
Smashed down every hovel-door,
Blazed its gifts of death and blood
Across the rubble and the mud;
Hark! the herald bombs declare
Hate, and woe, and deep despair!

No joy for me this Christmastide,
While children die, slow-crucified;
Ignorance alone is bliss –
And yet, I shall remember this:
Jesus came, the one true Way,
And on this glad and generous Day
There's hope the world may learn to prize
The light in Christmas-morning eyes.

WHAT IS CHRISTMAS?

Not turkey and trimmings
On a sumptuous table –
But a little brown baby
Born in a stable.

Not mountainous puddings
And heaps of mince pies –
But the motherhood glow
In a Jewish girl's eyes.

Not crackers and candles
And cakes richly iced –
But the humble appearing
Of Jesus, the Christ.

Beware of abundance!
Remember how odd
That an inn full of feasting
Had no room for God.

Christmas means caring,
And tasting afresh
The thrill of believing
That God became flesh.

IN-BETWEEN

Christmas in the olden days,
If we but knew our history,
Was mostly on a modest scale,
A deep religious mystery;
Folk of old would be amazed
To see the way we celebrate:
All the finest food and drink
That stomachs can accommodate;
And kindness shown to all around,
Effusive in our charity . . .
And yet our ancestors might claim
To see with stringent clarity,
That modern Nowells stand alone,
Quite freakish things, once-yearly seen,
One generous gush – and little left
For Christmas kindness in-between.

FIVE LITTLE FINGERS

Perfect new-born baby
From head to tiny toes
With five little fingers stretching
From out the swaddling clothes.
I love Studdert-Kennedy's thought,
Though some may think it odd,
When he sees in the hand of Jesus
'The Five Little Fingers of God'.

CHRISTIANS AWAKE!

A muffled assembling
On Christmas Eve:
Glimmers of torchlight,
A lantern held high,
As we stood by the cottage
Under star-frosted sky,
Waiting for midnight;
Our traditional first carol
A surprise long-expected –
On the first stroke of twelve:
'Christians, awake!'
Then on to wake others
All over the village,
Proclaiming a Saviour
To welcoming windows,
Invited indoors
For cake and mince pies
And hospitable warmth;
Then carolling forth
In the chill early hours . . .
Well, sleep through your Christmas,
But let me re-capture
That wide-awake rapture,
The tingle of singing
That all for our sake
The Christ-child is born,
As we set the stars ringing
With 'Hail! Smiling Morn!'
And the rare, youthful relish
Of Christians . . . awake!

NATIVITY PLAY

It *does* make you think, a Nativity Play!
How charming the children! And some folk would say:
All innocent, too, angelic, monastic . . .
But those humble Shepherds will soon be bombastic,
And the three generous Kings,
with offerings most rare,
Might grow up tight-fisted!
Who knows if they'll care
About worship and prayer
and devotion to God?
Our modern Wise Men
think such things quite odd . . .
On the other hand,
Herod might turn out quite well –
And those dear little Angels –
could give us all hell!
Will Joseph stay gentle,
and noble, and strong?
And Mary a Virgin?
Oh, I wonder how long!
Only the Baby will stay
just the same:
Familiar Stranger!
The Saviour who came
To share with poor mortals
a life now secure
From chances and changes –
all loving and pure
And innocent, too, if we follow his way –
A doll in a manger. But *he's* here to stay;
And when these sweet children are soured by age,
Will they turn for refreshment to this simple stage,
And glimpse through the cataract-blurrings of time
The clear, shining eyes of themselves – in their prime?

A CHRISTMAS CAROL

Tune: Benevento

Christians, sing and shout for joy!
Life begins in Bethlehem,
Blooms within this baby boy,
Flower of Jesse's noble stem,
Rose of Sharon, Prince of Peace,
All the grandest names are his,
All the honours heaven affords:
King of Kings and Lord of Lords!

Where, then, is the royal birth?
In a stable, dark and crude;
Walls of rock and floor of earth,
Unhygienic solitude;
Mary's love and Joseph's awe
Warm the babe amidst the straw;
How the Pharisees would scoff:
Cradled in a cattle-trough!

Amazing, unpretentious grace!
From the richest realms of bliss,
From beyond all time and space,
Humbled to be born like this!
How he stooped that he might be
Clothed in flesh and frailty:
Christ the common earth once trod,
Image of the hidden God.

Crowded from the busy inn,
Hounded south by Herod's men,
Burdened by the Cross of Sin,
Jesus was rejected then;
But we sing his welcome now,
Low before his cradle bow,
In our thankful hearts, O Lord,
Shall your Advent be adored.

CHRISTMAS HUMBUG

'Christmas is humbug!'
Said old Ebenezer –
But food's overflowing
From every fat freezer,
And drink's over-brimming
From bottle and barrel,
And atmosphere oozes
From candle and carol,
And such is our fill
Of Dickensian pleasure
That past comprehension
Are those who would measure
Our lordly indulgence;
Expenses are huge –
And we don't care a crumb
For pathetic old Scrooge . . .
But pause in your pleasures;
The context is grim:
See in his thousands
The *real* Tiny Tim,
The sick and the starving
Who cry in the night . . .
Hypocrites all of us!
Scrooge was dead right!
Christ came to teach us
Compassion and sharing:
Away with all humbug!
Christmas means caring.

CHRISTMAS ORDERS

A mother now stands with her bold little boy
In front of a Christmas shop-window display,
As he loftily points to each gleaming new toy
With which he fancies he'd like to play;
'I want one o' those! And the other, as well –
No! That one you promised me, right at the back;'
And he greedily adds to his list of desires
Enough to inflate a whole Santa Claus sack . . .

Oh, how far we've come from the stockinged surprise
And the secrets that thrilled and would richly reward us;
The old folks may smile, but there's shock in their eyes:
A little lad giving his Christmas orders!

CHRISTMAS WRAPPINGS

Phoney Santa in the store,
With sack and paunch so full:
His bogus beard a mobile mask
Of two-faced cotton-wool.

Phoney Jesus, centre-piece
Of glossy decoration
In good-for-sales shop-window crib
Devoid of consecration.

And yet the proper Santa thrives
In each child who believes;
The living Jesus changes lives
On caring Christmas Eves.

Oh, lead us, Lord, from surface things
To truth beneath the trappings,
From token Christs and cardboard Kings –
Forgive our Christmas wrappings.

WHITE CHRISTMAS

Romantic white Christmas!
Nostalgia supreme;
So rare, yet so longed for,
A Bing Crosby dream.

White Christmas? Who knows?
But one thing's for sure:
No Christmas card scene
For the Friend of the poor.

No home full of comforts
All snug in the snow,
But the simplest of living
Few of us know.

Our cold northern Christmas –
Luxurious within,
Warm sunny Judaea –
No room at the inn.

Bethlehem-born,
He was one of the crowd,
Had no easy life
With the rich and the proud.

And if *this* is our *God*,
With his love and his light,
Who cares, in the brilliance,
Whether Christmas is white?

MAGNIFICAT

Christmas in Suburbia!
Come Christians all, let us indulge
In plump and succulent delights!
We'll feast until we start to bulge!

Christmas in a famine-camp!
No feasting here. With failing breath
They plead for piteous bowls of food
Amidst the encroaching stench of death.

Christmas in old Bethlehem!
Behold the cowshed King of Kings,
Of whom his mother Mary sang
'He'll fill the hungry with good things'!

Christmas in the Christian heart!
Oh, Man for Others, make me see
The anguish of all hungry folk,
And feed them, Lord – through such as me.

CHRISTMAS CACTUS

Bright beside the crib of Jesus
Christmas Cactus, faithful friend,
Now aflame with buds and flowers,
Blossoms surely without end!

Vivid crimson blooms abounding,
Arching down in rich cascades,
Here and there, a flower dying,
Withers, but it never fades.

Holly bears its berries early,
Christmas Roses bloom so late,
But you, old friend, have perfect timing,
Just as if you know the date.

Sentimental though my fancy,
The royal Child these flowers shall please:
For Solomon in all his glory
Was not arrayed like one of these.

CHRISTMAS DREAM

Hassle, bustle,
Parcel-tussle,
Whopping shopping,
Present swapping,
Baking, caking,
Mince-pie-making,
Posting, hosting,
Turkey-roasting,
Greeting, treating,
Over-eating,
Lunching, munching,
Telly-hunching,
Drowsing, dozing,
Eyelids closing . . .

Now the dreaming:
Stars all gleaming,
Angels singing,
Gospel-bringing,
Baby-crying,
Manger-lying,
God descending
All-befriending,
Intervening –
That's the meaning –
Shepherds quaking,
Sheep forsaking –
For us, like them,
The time for waking.

A CHRISTMAS HYMN
Tune: Dix

Happy Christmas! Let us sing,
Celebrate the Saviour's birth!
Essence of the Unseen God
Gloriously revealed on earth,
Blazing into time and space,
Dazzling star of hope and grace!

Jesus born in Bethlehem,
Far away and long ago,
Ever-present in our hearts
Now your gentle beauty show,
Every weary life refresh,
Mighty Word in feeble flesh!

With the shepherds may we know
With the Wise Men may we see
Yearning, universal love
Cradled in simplicity,
Born that misery might cease,
Lord of life and Prince of Peace!

Through the glib, commercial blare
Of these overcrowded days
Let the joyful tidings sound
With authentic Gospel praise!
Mary's child, once born to bless,
Seal our Christmas happiness.

IT'S A BOY!

It's a Boy! It's a Boy!
Christmas morning, shout for joy!
Mary's baby's in the manger,
Welcome friend and welcome stranger!

Here is hope for mournful millions;
Now the world can start afresh.
Long awaited, the Messiah
Here at last in human flesh!

In this tiny new-born baby
Lies the strength of all the earth:
History will now be dated
From this simple, lowly birth.

Mystery of incarnation,
Living word of God above;
Prince of Peace shall be his title:
He will teach mankind to love.

Signal of our Christmas gladness
Bells of Bethlehem shall chime:
We will keep this glorious Birthday
Till the very end of time!

Mary's baby's in the manger,
Welcome friend and welcome stranger!
Christmas morning, shout for joy!
It's a Boy! It's a Boy!

GENTLE JESUS

Twelve million children a year still die of
hunger and preventable disease

Gentle Jesus, meek and mild,
What sentimental false veneer
Imagines that you might have smiled
To see our cosy Christmas cheer!

Gentle Jesus, meek and mild,
Homeless, ragged refugee!
Forgive us, festively beguiled,
For hearts grown hard with luxury.

Gentle Jesus, meek and mild,
Who came our famished souls to feed,
Let self-indulgence be reviled,
Turn inside out our generous greed!

Gentle Jesus, meek and mild,
We would your righteous anger learn,
For children starved, diseased, defiled,
With fierce protesting fury burn!

Ah! What a scandal if we fail
To feed a single starving child,
From Bethlehem we'll blaze a trail –
For gentle Jesus, meek and mild!

NAME THIS CHILD

*'Jesus Christ' is the Greek form of the
Hebrew 'Joshua, Messiah.'*

Warm upon a maiden's breast
A Jewish baby had been fed;
Reverently they gathered round:
'What's his name?' the shepherds said.

Joseph placed his rough-hewn hand
Upon the smooth and tender head;
'After Joshua we shall call him',
'A grand old name!' the shepherds said.

'Names,' said Joseph, 'must have meaning:
Bethlehem means The House of Bread;
Joshua means The Lord shall save us.'
'Glory to God!' the shepherds said.

Mary lifted gentle Joshua,
Laid him in his manger-bed:
'Here lies peace for all the earth.'
'The very words!' the shepherds said.

'Sleep, my Joshua, Hebrew baby;
From Bethlehem shall the world be fed;
But what strange name will Gentiles call him?'
'Jesus Christ,' the Wise Men said.

CLOSE ENCOUNTER

How readily the world believes
In other worlds in outer space,
And dreams up dazzling dynasties
Which far outshine the human race.

How seriously we take our myths
Of beings from bright galaxies,
Whose visits shall enlighten Earth
With transcendental mysteries.

What irony to miss the fact
Which dwarfs all science-fiction dreams:
The Word made flesh in Bethlehem:
Amazing fusion of extremes!

Incarnate God! From outer bliss
Our Time Lord has appeared on Earth!
And shepherds glimpse with breathless joy
The Close Encounter of his birth!

The awesome, luminescent skies
Proclaim the night of Love's descent,
And every faithful Christmas heart
Still warms with cosmic wonderment!

CHRISTMAS KITCHEN

Two more shopping days to go –
Lovely Christmas atmosphere!
Where's my idle husband gone?
'I'm tied up with the tinsel, dear!'
Come and help me stuff this turkey!
Give a hand with these mince pies!
Then we've got the cake to ice –
I wish you men would realise
That Christmas turns us into slaves,
We womenfolk who sweat away
In steaming hells of kitchen heat,
While you just wait for Christmas Day –
Quick! Spread this icing, while it's soft,
Then pipe on 'Xmas' in bright red,
And stick these little figures on –
Oh! Santa Claus has lost his head!
Pass the stuffing – watch the cat!
Forgot to turn the oven down –
I just can't do two things at once . . .

I thought my pies were nice and brown,
But look at this! It's all gone wrong!
The mincemeat's oozing out in driblets!
What a mess! – Oh, Lord! The cat!
It's gone and gobbled up the giblets!
What shall I do for gravy now?
Oh, leave the cake till the icing's hard!
Answer the phone! Answer the door!
We've forgotten to send the Smiths a card!
Where are the dates, and the figs, and the nuts?
I've run out of sugar – I've not got a scrap,
And the Sellotape's down to half an inch,
And all those presents still to wrap!

So temperatures and tempers rise . . .
Till peace on earth seeks armistice,
And, truce beneath the mistletoe,
We share a tasty Christmas kiss.

ONCE A YEAR

Christmas spirit! Sharp reminder
You and I could be much kinder:
Love should last the whole year through
Not a fussy day or two.

Holy Spirit! Wake and warm us!
Babe of Bethlehem transform us!
Word made flesh, so close, so clear!
Not a glimpse just once a year.

HERE ON EARTH

Mary's pain,
Mary's joy,
Mary's glory:
It's a Boy!

Dark December
Flares with light:
Little Jesus
Born tonight!

Hold him warmly,
Softly kiss
New-born flesh,
The dawn of bliss!

Life and love
Supremely given:
Here on earth
A pledge of heaven!

SANTA'S LAMENT

'Can't be done!' said old Santa Claus one winter night
'To take gifts to each child on the earth;
Though I'm fully aware that it's proper and right
And worthy of this unique birth.

'On half of the children I lavish my toys –
Stockings, pillow-cases, filled fit to burst;
The other half get simply nothing at all
But a helping of hunger and thirst.

'It's not time and transport – I've got magical means:
In two places at once is my style!
A billion visits, all on Christmas Eve,
No problem – and so worth my while.

'It's the *money*, you see. I'm short of hard cash;
That's why there's not a fair share;
So the world's better-off see their children's delight,
And the poor see their children's despair.

'Father Christmas, you call me, so caring and kind!
Bright herald of our gracious Lord!
But when millions of children are just left to die
Your Santa's a scandalous fraud!

'So, one of two things: either generously give,
And work till there's no child who starves;
Or pull off my beard, and spare me the shame
Of a Santa who does things by halves!'

BAD NEWS AT CHRISTMAS

Bad news like this is always hard to bear!
Hard at any time, but cruel at Christmas;
It slashes through our man-made calendar,
Scorning all our planned festivities,
Thrusting upon us this untimely heartache,
Seeming worse by contrast with rejoicing,
Crumpling the pleasing sentimental picture
Of Christmas spent in worldwide harmony,
With families gathered in their cosy homes,
Secure within the glow of heart's content . . .
The 1914 troops had truce at Christmas,
But onslaughts on the human mind and frame
Wage ceaseless war – and though angelic choirs
Goodwill from God and peace on earth proclaim,
We walking wounded limp through Yule-tide dazed,
And, draped in tinsel, shell-shocked, stand amazed;
'Cheer up!' they say. 'It's Christmas!' On they go,
Embarrassed by our non-participation – just as though
They think that we can switch from gloom to joy,
And by sheer force of will annul the facts
Which choke our appetite for food or fun . . .
Then shall we – just to please them – bravely smile
And go through all the motions of delight,
Munch our ritual turkey, mouth our pudding,
Grotesquely wear a mocking paper hat?
Yes! Why not? And far from looking on,
Uncomprehending watchers from outside,
We'll enter deeply into Christmas truth,
See the Mother bear her first-born Son
In that shabby man-forsaken stable,
See the family flee as refugees,
And Mary glimpse afar the looming Cross . . .

For Christmas joy was born from harsh despair,
The blazing love shone out from hopeless dark,
In naked, pain-prone flesh was God revealed:
Good tidings of great joy to sweeten grief!
Then round his manger-bed we'll seek relief,
Warmed by his grace, our melting sorrows yield.

FAIRY-TALE NATIVITY

We've glamorised his birth,
We've prettified his crib:
A fairy-tale nativity –
The annual Christmas fib.

This year we'll face the facts,
And in the Gospels read
Of Jesus born in poverty,
Identified with need.

Our self-destructing world
Cries out for saving grace:
Then see this Judge of all the earth,
Who wears a human face.

Let warring men beware!
Let violence be reviled!
You yet shall know the wrath of God
For every suffering child.

To shame us into love
The Lord of loving came:
Oh, would some spark of Christmas truth
Now set our hearts aflame!

WHO IS THIS?

Set to music for choir and orchestra by Martin Hotton

Who is this? Who is this?
Tiny baby in the straw!
He's the new-born son of Mary:
With the shepherds closer draw:
Cradled there so calm and neat,
See his perfect hands and feet,
Fragrant skin more soft than silk,
Dainty mouth all moist with milk;
Gaze upon his tender flesh,
Nurse him in a warm caress,
Gently hold his infant frame:
Little Jesus is his name!
Who is this? Who is this?
Little Jesus is his name!

Who is this? Who is this?
Tiny baby in the straw!
He'll grow up a Jewish preacher
Done to death by Roman law:
Flog him at the judgment seat!
Hammer through his hands and feet!
Nail his flesh to brutal wood!
Mocked, maligned, misunderstood;
Wide outstretched his bleeding hands
Where an anguished mother stands –
At thirty-three your son has died:
A carpenter is crucified!
Who is this? Who is this?
A carpenter is crucified!

Who is this? Who is this?
Tiny baby in the straw!
This is Christ, the Light Eternal,
He whom ancient prophets saw:
God in Bethlehem revealed!
See in helpless flesh concealed
Might and majesty and grace!
Saviour of the human race!
Soaring angels glory sing,
Round the world our carols ring
Till the earth with heaven accords:
King of Kings and Lord of Lords!
Who is this? Who is this?
King of Kings and Lord of Lords!

MADONNA AND CHILD

Why is he crying, this babe at the breast?
Mary has fed him, and now he should sleep;
There, there, little Jesus! Oh, why so distressed?
So cosy and comforted, why should you weep?

He weeps for the world in its hardness and greed,
For heartbroken mothers whose breasts cannot feed,
For the pampered abundance that turns a blind eye
To the starved Christmas babies too weak to cry.

A VERY SPECIAL JEW

During the census ordered by Caesar Augustus did some Roman
soldier on duty in Bethlehem record the birth of Jesus?

Another birth,
Another brat,
Another mouth to feed!
It's 'ard to tell
Just who's begat,
The way these blighters breed!
Now 'ere's a lass from Nazareth –
Too poor to rent a bed:
Her baby's in this cattle-trough,
With straw beneath 'is 'ead . . .
Oh add 'im to the census list,
Another bloomin' Jew . . .
If I were Caesar back in Rome
I know what *I* would do:
I'd crucify the blinkin' lot –
Still . . . he's a bonny little lad;
This one might be different . . .
And crucifixion's bad . . .
I didn't mean it, little man,
We'd not do that to *you* –
We'll note it on the census form:
A Very Special Jew.

CHRISTMAS SPIRIT

Our spirit comes in bottles
Of alcoholic bliss:
And sprigs of mystic mistletoe
Shall seal it with a kiss!
So here's to jolly Bacchus!
And Saturnalian mirth!
For with the pagan Romans
We'll soon be down to earth!

Our Spirit comes in carols
Of everlasting cheer:
For God is now Emmanuel,
Compassionately near:
So here's to gentle Jesus!
In Christ is all forgiven,
And with his herald angels
We'll sing our way to heaven!

GOOD OLD SAINT NICHOLAS!

Set to music for junior choir and orchestra by Martin Hotton

Good old Saint Nicholas
Who did good by stealth:
He crept round the houses
Distributing wealth!

Chorus
Oh, let's not be greedy!
We'll share with the needy,
Give more than we get
For the best Christmas yet!

The Bishop of Myra
Was Santa's real name,
And three golden sovereigns
That brought him to fame.

Now, three poor young maidens
Saint Nicholas did spy
A-hanging their stockings
Round the fireplace to dry.

In the dead of the night-time
When the fireplace was cold
He dropped down the chimney
His three coins of gold.

They fell in the stockings
While the poor maidens dreamed,
And on Christmas morning
Like magic it seemed!

Jolly Saint Nicholas,
Just one of his pranks –
He gave nice surprises
And wanted no thanks.

Still filling stockings,
Behind each good cause,
Is the red-hooded bishop
We call Santa Claus.

As happy as Santa
Are those who believe
That it's better to give – *(pause)*
Than it is to receive.

Chorus
Oh, let's not be greedy!
We'll share with the needy,
Give more than we get
For the best Christmas yet!

(The delightful music for this song is available from the author via the publishers)

KINGDOM COME

What's Christmas mean, if we stop to think?
Think of the wars and the terrorist bids,
Think of the slums and shanty towns,
And umpteen million half-starved kids!

The contrast kills my appetite
For luscious food on plates piled high:
The irony of festive bliss
If we'll but turn a bleary eye!

Two worlds apart – yet linked by this:
God on earth to reconcile,
The loving, saving Prince of Peace,
Who bids us celebrate in style.

Then keep with Christ his rightful feast,
Anticipate a world set free
To eat its fill and share its joys –
Christmas is how it's *going* to be!

LOOK CLOSE THIS CHRISTMAS

Beneath commercial Christmas wrappings,
The standardised and tinselled trappings,
Beneath the layers of long tradition
And haze of pagan superstition,
Submerged beneath the drink and food,
Romantically misconstrued,
See a new-born baby boy . . .
Look closer still:
More deeply wrapped
In tiny frame
Of puny flesh,
See the everlasting flame
Of pure transcendent love,
The vast, all-cheering glow
Of God's goodwill,
And starry skies
Ablaze with joy!

YORKSHIRE CHRISTMAS

(In West Riding dialect)

Christmas in t' farm-'ouse,
All fettled an' clean:
Ther's a feast on yon table
'At's fit for a queen;
A gurt buxom turkey
Wi' t' trimmin's ter come,
An' a champion puddin',
An' sauce laced wi' rum;
Aye, ther's cheese, an' ther's spice-cake
An' summat ter sup –
By gum, lad, tha'll bust
If tha doesn't give up!

Christmas in t' mistal,
All shabby an' bare,
All stinkin' wi' cow-muck,
An' t' cattle just stare,
As much as ter say:
'There's nowt 'ere for thee!'
But ovver in t' corner . . .
Na then – dosta see?
Ther's a lass wi' 'er babby,
All snuggled in t' 'ay:
Yon grand little Jesus
On t' first Christmas Day!

PATIENT'S CHRISTMAS

Christmas in hospital,
Nurses to cheer you;
Bed-bound at home,
The family all near you . . .
Yet the sick and the suffering
May find little ease
In seasonal high spirits
Intended to please;
No well-meaning jollity
Brightening the bed
Can soothe troubled minds
Or drive out the dread . . .
But the hope and the joy
The carols proclaim,
Nourish and strengthen
Our spiritual frame:
The essence of Christmas
Is all things made new –
The life beyond dying,
Brought into view;
And the pain and the sorrow
We may yet transcend
Through the Christmas good tidings
That God is our Friend.

TWO DONKEYS

(Written for one of our grandchildren)

I am the Donkey of Mary;
Together we've travelled the road,
With Joseph leading us southwards,
And me gladly bearing the load.

I'm proud to have carried this lady,
And now that we're both safely here,
She lies in the straw, close beside me:
I've told her there's nothing to fear . . .

I was the same with *my* first-born;
There's always the pain and the danger . . .
Ah, it's over – a fine-looking baby –
And she's laying him down in my manger!

We donkeys, you know, have our feelings,
Though folk think we're slow and contrary,
And I feel so proud and so honoured,
For I am the Donkey of Mary.

And yet, when this child grows to manhood,
I know what would give me most pride:
Oh, how I shall envy the donkey
Who'll one day give *Jesus* a ride!

CHRISTMAS QUARREL

We've had a lovely Christmas row!
Can't think how it arose –
A 'Hark the herald' shouting match:
We nearly came to blows.

One minute it was 'Silent night',
The next all hell let loose;
Instead of peace on earth we had
A battle of abuse.

Smouldering feelings had flared up,
Fanned by festive tension,
And blazed away with free advice
On things no-one should mention.

Goodwill to all, the angels sang,
And though they do know best,
It's good to clear the Christmas air
And get things off your chest.

To hear what others really think
Beneath their bonhomie
Is worth far more than all the gifts
Unwrapped with pseudo-glee.

Who gave us what a year from now,
We'll scarcely recollect –
But not the Christmas when we weren't
Politically correct!

CASHING IN ON CHRISTMAS

Sung to 'Jingle Bells'

Struggling through the crowds,
Roaming round the town,
All this Christmas shopping – oh!
It really gets you down!
Your corns and bunions twinge,
Your poor feet swell and ache,
You clutch at awkward parcels
Till you feel your arms'll break . . .

Chorus
Oh! Jingle bells! Jingle bells!
Join the jamboree!
We're going Christmas crackers,
In a mammoth spending-spree!
Oh! Jingle bells! Jingle bells!
Money in the till!
We're cashing in on Christmas –
It's the season of goodwill!

It's murder in the shops,
It's slaughter in the stores –
You're squashed in escalators
And you're mangled in the doors;
Yet you never feel the wounds,
While the battle's on:
They bleed you dry, and then you cry:
'Oh, where's the money gone?'!

Chorus

Some soap for Auntie Jane,
A tie for Uncle Jack –
We know he'll never wear it,
But he buys us something back;
And as for Cousin Fred,
That's two years now he's missed,
Where's your Christmas spirit, Fred? –
Oh, cross him off the list!

54

Chorus

We've spent so much this time,
Far more than we ought –
It's not the gift that counts, of course,
It's really just the thought –
But they'd better buy for us
Something just as dear –
If not – you bet – we shan't forget
When Christmas comes next year!

Chorus

PREACHER'S CHRISTMAS

What shall we preach this Christmas-time?
Something relevant and fresh!
Preach the ancient Gospel story,
Preach the Word revealed in flesh,
How the earth was touched with glory,
How the unseen God appeared,
How the heavens blazed in splendour,
How the awe-struck shepherds feared,
How they found a new-born baby,
Saw the cosmic master-plan:

Loving, healing, saving Jesus,
Paradox of God made man!

The old, old story, ever new . . .
The merest carol makes us think!
And one rich ounce of Christmas truth
Outweighs the tons of food and drink;
Then seek no more some brave new theme:
Preach God in Christ – the text supreme.

CAROL SINGERS

Children's off-key cheeky voices
Serenading Hobson's choices,
Carol singers! Not again!
God rest you merry gentlemen!

What a two-faced Christmas racket!
Out of tune, but well in pocket;
Doorstep duos none can quell,
Fingers poised to press the bell!

Hear their breathless, gabbled greetings,
Door-to-door their brisk repeatings;
Festive blackmail! Who could doubt it?
What would Christmas be without it?

Ah, now we know . . . The streets today,
No longer safe for kids to play,
Doors unopened, bells unrung –
And not a single carol sung.

AN OLD-FASHIONED CHRISTMAS

A sentimental song

Christmas is the loveliest time,
The happy ending of the year,
And you and I must guard it well
Lest old customs disappear.

Chorus
Oh, for an old-fashioned Christmas,
Like those we can recall:
When in the cosy firelight
The little children's eyes are bright,
As snowflakes lightly fall;
The lights are on the Christmas tree,
There's welcome, cheery company –
Let's have an old-fashioned Christmas,
The nicest one of all!

Let's keep Christmas evergreen,
With glossy holly, berries bright;
Hang a bunch of mistletoe –
Not too obviously in sight!

Chorus

The sparkle of the Christmas tree,
Shall fill the room with Yule-tide cheer,
The cards upon the mantelpiece
Shall bring our distant loved ones near.

Chorus

Thoughtful presents we'll exchange,
And heartily we all shall eat:
Candlelight shall touch with gold
Many a rich, traditional treat.

Chorus

Lively carols we shall sing,
Rejoicing in the Saviour's birth,
Sense a magic atmosphere,
Just a hint of heaven on earth!

Chorus

THE DEVIL'S KNELL

On Christmas Eve at Dewsbury
They toll the Devil's Knell,
To celebrate Old Nick's defeat
And keep him down in hell.

A peal for every year since Christ
They cheerfully discharge:
Oh, pull those bell-ropes harder, lads!
The Devil's still at large.

CHRISTMAS ROBIN

From rows of robins caged in cards
I turned and looked outside:
And there he was – near the window-pane,
With his dapper brown coat and russet breast,
Impeccably, handsomely, festively dressed,
So small, so proud, so self-possessed,
All bright and beady-eyed.

As cock-robins do, he cocked his head,
Almost as if to say:
'Now *I'm* for real, not imprisoned on card,
Out in the cold, but cheerfully free,
And all that I own is just what you see –
Do you think you could spare a crust for me
To celebrate this Day?'

'He *can't* know it's Christmas!' my reason rebuked,
'It's only by chance that he comes';
But out on the deep-frozen, hoar-frosted lawn
I rejoiced in this robin so warmly alive,
Who so opportunely had chanced to arrive,
And it made my day to know he would thrive
On a feast of Christmas crumbs.

And I thought of the presents we give and receive,
Exchanging by millions expensive amounts,
But my crumbs brought a pleasure you'd hardly believe:
With robins it's more than the thought that counts.

CHRISTMAS AIN'T WHAT IT USED TO BE

Christmas ain't what it used to be –
And it's not just a trick of the memory . . .

In far-away pre-electronic days
We sat round real fires, and basked in the blaze,
We stood round pianos, and carolled away,
We gathered round tables, a joy to survey –
Choicest home-cooking, home-baking, home-brewing,
Convivial feasting, with no-one half viewing,
Head-turning, neck-twisting, so anxious to see
The strident enticements of Yule-tide TV;
Instead of the non-stop compulsory screen
We'd the homely old wireless, with the King, then the Queen,
Speaking in person, uniting the nation,
And Commonwealth, too, in worldwide celebration;
While the kids on the hearthrug found simple delight
In the toys and the treats from the magical night
When stocking and pillowcase Santa Claus filled
And each young believer rewarded and thrilled . . .

But there's so much to *buy* now, such freedom to choose,
And superstores bursting with goodies and booze,
And TV commercials to speed up the shopping
For the annual madness of tit-for-tat swapping!
Gone crackers with spending, till royally sat,
We're appropriately crowned in a daft paper hat . . .

Oh it's bright and it's jolly – just as seen on TV . . .
But Christmas . . . ain't what it used to be.

THE UNNOTICED GUEST

By an Act of Parliament 1652 Christmas was abolished

'A plague on thy Christmas!'
The Puritans cried:
'Thou glutton! Thou drunkard!
Thy flesh-pots we've spied!
'Tis pagan, 'tis popish,
'Twill lead to damnation:
God cancels thy Christmas –
By State proclamation!'

A Christ without Christmas?
He calls us to dine!
He feeds the five thousand,
Turns water to wine,
Sits down at the tables
Of commonplace sinners:
The unnoticed Guest
At all Christmas dinners.

So eat and be merry!
Rejoice in his birth!
Let feasting, not fasting,
Replenish the earth!
But share with the hungry,
Keep Jesus in sight:
For a Christmas that's Christ-less
Proves the Puritans right.

CHRISTMAS PUDDING

A magnificent dinner –
Crowned by this pudding
So rich and spicy,
Robed in rum sauce! . . .

Millions of children
Go without dinner,
Not just at Christmas,

No dinner ever –
Nothing to speak of,
Square meals unheard of,
They'd eat up the scraps,
The crumbs from our tables;
Picture those children
Crying for feeding,
Aching with hunger,
Dying of famine –
Shocking! Oh, shocking!

Any more pudding?

ODE ON THE NATIVITY

In the style of Milton

Hail, festival supreme,
The pantomimic scheme
Of ancient winter-solstice pagan rites,
The Saturnalian kiss,
The Bacchanalian bliss
Of drowsy days and bright, carousing nights!
And can this brash and earth-bound thing
Proclaim old Milton's infant God and heavenly King?

The Jesus pot-pourri,
Messiah's spending-spree –
Thou, Milton, shouldst be living at this hour!
The self-indulgent zeal,
The wealth that will not feel
The pain of hungry millions who'd devour
Our very Christmas scraps and crumbs,
While telly kindly screens from sight their alien slums.

And yet we shall transcend
This pagan-Christian blend,
Away with bogus Yule-tide bonhomie!
And let us taste afresh
The truth of God made flesh,
And celebrate the Christ who sets us free;
Though we are Puritans no more,
With Milton let us open wide the stable door.

CHRISTMAS TEARS

An empty chair this Christmas
An absent voice and face,
A chill amidst the festive warmth,
A stark and haunting space.

How shall we curb our grieving?
The pain grows keener yet;
The all-contrasting cheer ensures
That no-one can forget.

But blessèd are the mourners
Who through the darkness grope
To find their comfort at the crib,
Where lies the Lord of hope.

Behold the bright Madonna!
Behold her baby's charms!
And glimpse beneath our fragile world
The everlasting arms!

O God of signs and wonders,
Now let this new-born boy
Transmute our very tears of grief
To Christmas tears of joy!

TALKIN' TURKEY

In East Riding dialect

Di yer knaw 'at Kessmas turkey,
T' nation's fav'rite champion rooast,
A long while sin' – i' Tudor times –
Cem ti roost on t' Yorkshire cooast?

It's reight, yer knaw – a Boynton feller –
William Strickland, sooa the' say,
Browt t' fost bods frev ower t' ooacean,
Ti Bollinton's 'istoric Bay.

'E'd copped a feew i' t' brave Neew World,
To wheear 'e'd saailed wi' young Cabot,
'E thowt: 'The'll breed, an' fetten up,
An' grandish taaste, when pipin' 'ot!'

'E landed 'at Brid, an' took 'is bods
Ti Boynton village, just clooase by;
In t' choch ther's a turkey carved – i' wood –
Ah bet ther's fooaks oft wondered why.

Well, seean the' spread all ower t' kingdom,
Caught on saame as Yorksher Pud –
But sooth o' t' booarder thoo'll neean taaste
Puds ner turkeys *awf* as good!

Beware o' suthern imitaations!
Proper Puddin's 'ard ti mak:
All yon sad an' soggy dollops –
Yan cannot stomach sike poor tack!

It's t' saame wi' t' turkey – cook it *slowly,*
Baaste yon breast wi' lovin' care;
Then give it t' prahde o' place on t' taable:
Traditional, 'olesome *Yorksher* fare!

Ah'm capped 'at Strickland's neean got credit
For t' Kessmas culinary tops –
Just leeak at yond! All gowlden broon:
Bah, ther's slavver runnin' doon mi chops!

Ah'll carve a slahce or two for thoo, lad,
Wi' steamin' stuffin; from t' insahde –
An t' best of all yer taasty tthrimmins –
Just a dash o' Yorksher prahde!

HOW MANY TURKEYS?

Every Christmas twelve million turkeys are eaten in Britain

How many turkeys will it take?
How many tons of Christmas cake?
How many million hot mince pies?
Before the world will realise
The meaning of the Incarnation:

Peace for every violent nation,
Food for every starving child,
Love for the unreconciled,
Hope for those whom none console,
God for every searching soul!

Forgive us, Lord, that we are blind:
We dwarf your truth by being kind,
Glimpse not your Cross through thoughtless ease,
Nor see the wood for Christmas trees.

How long shall we confine his Birth?
O Christmas Kingdom, come on earth!
Triumphantly from Bethlehem break!

How many turkeys will it take?

XMAS

There is a curious Christian myth
Which says you musn't use
The shortened form of 'Xmas':
I know some who refuse:
It's wrong to leave out Christ, they say,
It's modern, slick, commercial . . .
But here's a bit of history,
By no means controversial:
X is simply Greek 'CH',
An old abbreviation:
Christ's in 'Xmas' – more, in fact,
Than in our celebration.

DARK SIDE OF CHRISTMAS

The golden Christmas candle cheers –
Yet sheds its silent, molten tears;
The holly cordially adorns –
Yet bares those stark and hostile thorns;
The royal Babe of Virgin bride –
Is crowned with thorns, and crucified . . .
And Christmas cheer, however bright,
Is set in sombre shades of night;
Behind the front of festive pride
Each Christmas has a darker side . . .
Our mounds of food cannot conceal
The scandalous Third World beggar's meal;
Our luxuries cannot obscure
The starved and shrivelled, hopeless poor;
Our season's glow of warm goodwill
Is mocked by millions trained to kill . . .
O Word made flesh, the one true Light,
Shine forth afresh in our dark night!
Teach us your caring, sharing way
Till the wide world dawns to Christmas Day!

HOLY FAMILY

This is the feast of families,
When prodigals return,
And fathers kill the fatted calf,
And mothers quickly learn
All the secret hopes and fears
Of daughter and of son,
And home's a place of honest love
Whatever's said or done.

Thank God for close-knit families –
But think of those dispersed
By shabby deeds and bitter words
That cannot be reversed;
Where flesh and blood is torn by strife
How keen the Christmas grieving:
That broken homes should heal again
Seems quite beyond believing.

Yet see the Holy Family
With hope for all the earth,
And healing, reconciling love,
Outflowing from this birth:
O isolated hearts grown cold,
You may by Christ be warmed,
And leave this nuclear-family scene
Inspired, refreshed, transformed!

A KILLING AT CHRISTMAS

For its Christmas dinner
Our cat killed a robin –
Then disdained to eat it;
The soft-feathered corpse
In its minuscule grave
Spoiled my own appetite . . .

Even at Christmas
There's bloodshed and loss,
Even in Bethlehem,
We're close to the Cross . . .
And that's where the robin,
So folklore maintains,
As it comforted Christ,
Caught its red stains –
A gory reminder,
Though the table is set,
That there's killing at Christmas,
While we feast and forget.

ELECTRONIC CHRISTMAS

Come, ye faithful telly-gawpers!
Gather round the potent screen,
Addicts all of non-stop viewing,
Keep the Christmas quarantine!

What if what we see is rubbish?
Drugged and mesmerised we gaze . . .
Oh, kick the glued-to-telly habit,
Break the bleary-eyed malaise!

Switch your mind to gaze and ponder
On a certain starry night:
When the little Lord of glory
Came to flood the world with light.

Electronic, man-made Christmas!
So much there so false and glib;
View, this once, the God-made channel:
Gather round the Christmas crib!

COLD-SHOULDER CHRISTMAS

Little old lady, all alone,
Sad Yule-tide monologue:
She'll not see a soul all Christmas,
Except for her little dog.

Dogs don't have souls, I hear you say;
They do when you live alone,
When the Christmas box that pleases most
Is a tail-wagging, juicy bone.

Nobody cares enough to call,
And all that will make her rejoice
Is the look on the face of a mongrel dog,
At the sound of his mistress's voice.

Was Jesus not born to teach us love,
And make us good neighbours and friends?
Then shame on a cold-shoulder Christmas,
When even a dog comprehends!

BETHLEHEM PILGRIMAGE

Written following a visit to the Church of the Holy Nativity in Bethlehem, when the poet noticed Arab Christian children walking through the very low doorway.

To see the place where Christ was born
You have to stoop so low!
Through tiny door and gloomy cave
The humbled pilgrims go,
Then crouch to touch the silver star
That marks the very place
Where Mary bore the unique flesh,
The fount of truth and grace . . .
The children freely enter in,
No need have *they* to bend;
But we are old in years and sin,
And need to comprehend
That Bethlehem leaves no place for pride:
The God of starry skies
Has touched the earth in tender love –
And cut us down to size!
How vain the Christmas spending-spree,
The over-lavish table!
God works through simple souls who see
A baby in a stable.

WHEN I BELIEVED IN SANTA CLAUS

When I believed in Santa Claus,
I'd go to bed devoutly thrilled,
In sure and certain Christmas hope
Of stocking and pillow-case lavishly filled.

Then at some pitch-black freezing hour
I'd wake to feel with blissful feet
The magic burden on the bed –
Oh, spine-tingling, ravishing Santa Claus treat!

'He's been!' came a whisper through the dark,
But I'd tell my young brother that Dad said to wait,
And we'd drift into a luxurious sleep,
To dream of delight at a quarter to eight.

And at the merest hint of dawn
We'd extricate treasures with whoops of pure joy:
An apple, an orange, new penny, much more –
And the special, long hoped-for, heart-throbbing toy!

Ah! Tender the memories of all that I miss,
As life to its swift conclusion draws;
And best of a thousand thrills of bliss:
When I believed in Santa Claus!

COMPULSORY CHRISTMAS

Christmas is compulsory,
You simply can't avoid it . . .
Though Cromwell's Puritans once thought
They'd finally destroyed it,
And banned the feast perpetually
In Sixteen Fifty-Two,
Effaced all trace of Christmas grace
From public house to pew,
And though their Act of Parliament
Has never been repealed,
The fate of festive abstinence
Was soon for ever sealed,
For Dickens made a new decree,
That henceforth no-one dare
Abstain like Ebenezer Scrooge
From Christmas fun and fare:
You *must* join in the jollity,
No matter what you're feeling,
With smiling Christmas-wrapper face
The honest truth concealing;
You may be low and close to tears,
Immersed in personal sadness,
But now by international law
You'll feign appropriate gladness:
Christmas is compulsory
And nothing can destroy it –
So since it's inescapable
We might as well enjoy it!

HAPPY BIRTHDAY, JESUS!

Join the Jesus birthday party!
Universal Yule-tide cheer,
Lakes of liquor, punch and wine
And ever-flowing beer;
Tons of turkey, pork and ham,
Mountains of mince pies,
Piles of richest Christmas pud –
So come and feast your eyes,
And fill yourself until you burst,
And slake your alcoholic thirst,
And sport a Christmas-cracker hat,
Then take your ease, and doze or chat,
With tinselled tree and pretty cards
Surrounding you with kind regards;
Then Christmas birthday cake and cheese,
And nuts and fruit and whatever you please . . .

In fact, too much upon your plate
To think whose birth you celebrate:
Royal guests who've quite expelled
The one for whom the party's held,
And like the crowded inn of old
Keep the King . . . out in the cold.

WESLEY'S CHRISTMAS

John Wesley joined our Christmas Day,
Cried out in consternation:
'Is this not just like heathen Rome?
'Tis nought but dissipation!
Worldly goods are all I see,
No Gospel grace for sinners,
Nor even grace when you sit down
To eat your Christmas dinners!
You serve the god of Mammon still,
With gifts to one another,
And scorn to feed the hungry poor,
Your sister and your brother,
For whom the Saviour came to die –'

Yet when he looked more closely,
He saw such intermingled good,
And said, far less morosely:
''Tis true, I own, that some there are
Who live this day in love,
And keep the feast with prayer and praise,
Their minds on things above,
And hark! They sing with brother Charles
Of peace and mercy mild,
Proclaim that Best of All, our God
Is with us – as a Child . . .'
So, quoting these, his dying words,
John Wesley rode away,
Glad of hearts still strangely warmed
By every Christmas Day.

BREATHALYSER

Christmas spirit poured from bottles:
Drown your cares in demon drink!
Just another for the road, now –
Always later than you think!

Demon drink for demon drivers:
Have another, don't be shy:
Now the Christmas lights are twinkling
In each boozy, bloodshot eye.

Who shall curb convivial freedom?
Spoilsports all who say us nay –
Till the sobered flesh lies throbbing,
Slaughtered on the motorway.

Till the driver, though surviving,
Smashes someone else to death;
Tragic, wicked, bloody Christmas:
Horror held within a breath!

NEW BABY

Any tiny baby you may see
Snuggled cosy-close on mother's knee
Is guaranteed to raise a tender 'Ah!'
Instinctively we stoop to smile and gaze
And babble baby-talk in lavish praise,
As quite befits this brave new infant star.

But what if we had seen at Mary's breast
Her tiny new-born baby warmly pressed?
What then?! Oh, we'd have held our breath for joy,
Stunned to silence by this unique birth,
Inadequate to praise the awesome worth
Of Bethlehem's once-and-only baby boy.

Though every child's miraculously made,
With charms that even atheists persuade,
And moves to tears all but the living dead,
No birth or baby ever yet beguiled
Like that far-off familiar Christmas child,
With untold millions round his makeshift bed.

JEHOVAH'S CHRISTMAS

Strange Jehovah's Witness:
Christ without a Christmas!
But, worse, the world enticed
By Christmas without Christ!
Winter solstice revels
Still favour festive devils:
The gods of pagan Yule,
The wild Lords of Misrule,
The jolly drunken drivers
Embracing their survivors . . .
Scenes where pagan Rome
Would feel so much at home,
Where many Christians might
Say the Witnesses are right!
And yet the heathen basis
Provides a rare oasis,
Where humans winter-weary
Hear carols ever-cheery,
Their news unique: a birth
To save the woeful earth . . .
Though Christ is ostracised,
The world's evangelised,
Offered a brand new start:
This Child can touch the heart . . .

Then Christmas let us keep;
The time is growing shorter:
Don't throw *this* Baby out
With the modernised,
Mythologised,
Re-paganised,
Commercialised,
Bath water.

GIVING

The world goes mad at Christmas,
Forgets its strife and sorrow;
And spends and spends and spends again,
As if there's no tomorrow.

More money spent at Christmas
Than throughout all the year
On cards and food and glossy gifts,
On spirits, wine and beer.

And though it's true a little, too,
Is given to the needy,
More is spent upon ourselves
And affluence makes us greedy.

Yes. Buy me this, and buy me that –
I'll buy you something back:
A self-indulgent present-swap
For all who've got the knack.

And yet, how odd it is that God
Should give – and risk such loss:
Birth in a stable, life on the roads,
And death on a cruel Cross.

But that, of course, is *giving*:
It puts *our* gifts to shame;
For God so loved he gave himself
And flesh and blood became.

And came to show that here below
What makes life worth the living
Is not some lottery win of wealth,
But glad and gracious giving.

CHRISTMAS CONSERVATION

Christmas in the Dales!
The children all agog
Round blazing hearth of festive flames
And ancient Yule-tide log;
And there, across the yard,
The Christ-child's lowly stable,
And round our fire a rural peace,
And on our plenteous table
Christmas cake, custom-baked,
Married to Wensleydale cheese . . .

Such simple things are all we need
To set the heart at ease –
But, country folk, beware
An invader who shows no pity:
If *telly* rules Christmas you might as well be
Deep in some drab inner city!

CHRISTMAS VISITS

'Nice to see you! Glad you've come!'
The greetings sound sincere:
But inwardly there must be some
Who wish their guests weren't here.

We're social beings, yet we tire
Of over-population;
Space and time we all require
And room for relaxation.

Yet though we'd like a bit of peace,
Our cosy home's precarious:
Like cackling, fattening Christmas geese
We've got to be gregarious.

But let's make Yule-tide welcomes bright,
Our pleasure frankly showing:
Just think of this: the sheer delight
Of when we see them going!

COWS AT CHRISTMAS

Christmas! Pagan in all but name:
The Mass of Christ, the Word made flesh . . .
These days, who cares?
Oh, yes! Carol tunes for atmosphere,
Electronically mass-produced
To gild commercial cake,
A pseudo-Christian veneer
On heathen winter rites . . .
Yet, in the country,
On starry nights,
It's more like pastoral Palestine,
And here, in this cowshed,
It's as though the very beasts
Remember in some strange way
The Child born close,
In the smell of dung and hay,
With shepherds, practical men,
And the Magi, academics,
United in adoration . . .
Yes! For a whiff of Christmas,
I'll make new pilgrim vows,
Escape from the telly,
Tyrannical festive chatterbox,
And slip away to the mistal
To ruminate alone
With simple Christmas cows.

CLOUDED CHRISTMAS

Have you seen the news?
Only brute beasts, the ox and the ass,
Can know contentment at Christmas;
For humans, who think, and feel, and remember,
What sorrows now rush in upon us!
The accidents, disasters, diseases,
The constant pelter of evil
That takes no Christmas break . . .
When I think of the bereaved, the maimed, the starving,
These rich delicacies stick in my throat . . .

But then I think of that *they* would wish:
'To share our grief,' they might say,
'Is to double it . . . Rejoice while you may:
Your turn is yet to come . . .
The very reason we weep
Is for lack of the good things you have:
Why should you waste them on our behalf?
Rather enjoy them all the more,
Make use of our very pain
To sharpen the edge of your appetite:
Eat, drink and be merry.
For tomorrow you too will die!'

Some folk, of course, don't give a damn,
And tuck in regardless;
But these are less than human,
Blinkered less-than-beasts,
Mere stomachs to be filled;
They miss this added savour
Of compassion and thanksgiving,
The subtle Christmas blend
That makes New Years worth living.

AUTHENTIC CHRISTMAS

Will *this* Christmas be like all the rest?
The frantic preparing and over-indulging,
Wallets all empty and paunches all bulging,
A phenomenon difficult to digest.

Oh, let it be deeper than layers of bright wrappings,
Far more than a flurry of Christmas-card caring,
Far more than a show of convivial sharing,
With carols and crib merely part of the trappings.

Let it be, as in days before consumer greed,
A simple, heartfelt thrill of wonder
That God should have torn the heavens asunder
And dwelt in flesh to meet our need!

SIMPLE THINGS

On seeing our grandchildren on Christmas morning
happily playing with a big cardboard box.

See the presents they've received
From Santa's cornucopian bag,
With all the doting mums and grans
Providing him with seasonal swag!
But, look! Their toys they cast aside,
Though all brand-new and orthodox,
And choose instead to romp and play
Within an empty cardboard box . . .
It's a house, or a boat, or whatever they please –
Imagination is the measure;
What Christmas price we pay to learn
That simple things give greatest pleasure!

GLORIA IN EXCELSIS

A snowball fight – outside a church:
Compacted hard as stone
Snowballs soar through icy air,
By strong-armed urchins thrown:
A smash of glass! The warriors flee;
Inside the church the vicar stops
His Christmas preparations,
And sees, aghast, the damage done:
Of all the desecrations
None worse than this! How sad to see
The beauteous stained-glass window marred:
The Christ-child's angel choirs!
A pane has gone – a gaping hole!
No message now inspires,
For 'Glory to God in the highest' reads,
With the letter E knocked out,
'Glory to God in the High-St(reet) . . .'
But these words have quite a clout;
The vicar looks, and feels inspired:
Here's a text on which he'll preach!
Let High Street air come into church,
And churches ever outwards reach,
And touch our streets with Christmas truth:
Glory to God throughout the town!
On every home and place of work
Let joyful tidings shimmer down;
No stained-glass God, unreal, remote,
But down to earth, involved in time,
Conveying through this quaint misquote
Celestial grace and love sublime:
From highest heaven to basest earth,
See Christ the Saviour-King descend!
This is the measure of his birth:
The Lord who loves us to the end;
No palace pleasures shall he know,
Nor cushioned comforts wealth can show,

Stable-born, the dust he'll tread:
The Sinner's Friend, who wept and bled;
Through crowded street and market place –
The God who wears a human face . . .

The vicar now is pleased to see
The fragments of his letter E;
So glad that God, on Christmas Days,
Still moves in such mysterious ways.

THREE O'CLOCK

It's three o'clock! Come gather round
This unique British paradox:
Her glorious Majesty the Queen
All gift-wrapped in a Christmas box.

George the Fifth and Sixth before
Through wireless sought their folk to reach;
The Queen now pops in every home
To give her after-dinner speech.

Republicans may switch her off
Or snooze with jocularity;
But, as for us, 'God save the Queen!'
And Christmas solidarity.

A CHRISTMAS CALVARY

Jesus Christ is crucified
Every Christmas Day;
The Saturnalian soldiers mock:
'You're not a King!' they say;
With holly as his Crown of Thorns,
And tinsel round his wrists,
They flog with Christmas cracker lash
And punch with pudding fists;
With mistletoe for Judas kiss,
And Pilate's clean-washed hands,
They now can do away with him,
And in all Christian lands
They string him up on Christmas trees,
And go their festive way –
Those, I mean, without a thought
Of who was born today . . .

A twisted irony of time,
Our Merry Christmas kills:
For if we fail to care and give
And act out our good wills,
And let this Jesus touch our hearts,
Then, once again, he'll be
The King they snubbed as they passed by –
A Christmas Calvary.

A BIT OF A CHANGE
In West Riding Dialect

A grand Christmas dinner wor sided at last –
Then they all started fratchin' away
Ovver t' programmes the' wanted on t' telly –
It wor ruinin' wer Christmas Day.

Some wanted *one* thing, an' some wanted t' other:
Young uns says, '*We'll* 'ave James Bond!
'Ah'll not stand fer that!' grandfatther says –
An' 'e likes 'is own way, does yond.

'Well, sit thissen dahn, then,' grandmother bawls,
'Cahr quiet, an' just clooase thi een!'
So, queer as Dick's 'atband, they all gathered rahnd,
Gawpin' all gawmless at t' screen.

The' switched t' blamed set on – but nowt 'appened –
The'd watch owt nah, on *that* they agreed,
But choose '*ah* the' brayed it an' pawsed it abaht
It wor plain 'at yon telly 'ad *deed*.

It wor like a bereavement in t' family, tha knaws:
Ivvery face wore a reight solemn frahn –
A gatherin' o' mawks i' daft comic 'ats –
'Eart-sluffened, 'cos t' telly'd brok dahn.

Well, wi lit a grand fire, wi' gurt blazin' logs,
Turned wer backs on t' blank, sackless screen,
An' wi switched on t' wireless at 3 o'clock,
An' just sat theeare an' listened ter t' Queen.

Then wi gat laikin' at cards – an' liked it, an' all –
It wor summat we'd not done fer years –
An' wi supped, an' wi kalled, rahnd yond fire –
Ah felt just like shahtin' three cheers!

Then wi sang a feew carols, an' talked of owld times,
An' passed rahnd all t' nuts, dates an' chocs –
Wi got on that *well* it left us fair capped –
An' we'd all brokken loose from yon box!

Tell thee t' treeuth, it wor t' best Christmas *ivver:*
Good company allus ameeuses –
An owld-fashioned Yule-tide, baht telly –
Ee . . . Ah'm reight glad Ah rived aht yon feeuses!

side clear away, *fratch* quarrel, *een* eyes, *bray* hit, *pawse* kick,
mawk sullen, unco-operative person, *'eart-sluffened* very upset
laik play, *kall* chat, *fair capped* really surprised, *baht* without.

MISTLETOE TRADITION

The Druids' sacred healing bough,
Cut with golden sickle:
Now reduced to an excuse
For giggling slap and tickle!

Mystic sprig of mistletoe
Suspended in the air;
We scarcely ever glance at it,
And yet we know it's there:
Licence for a little kiss
Or luscious osculation:
Ancient Celtic charm of love,
And modern medication . . .

When doctors bring
blood pressure down
Wonder drugs they'll try:
One comes from the magic berries
That send BP sky-high!
An English custom once, they say,
Which shocked our foreign friends:
Stolen kisses, none so sweet,
But that, of course, depends
On who is kissing who, and how –

And please don't overdo it:
Tradition's limit don't exceed,
Or you are sure to rue it:
One kiss allowed – no more, no less –
For each berry white and pearly,
And after each kiss a berry's plucked –
By those who get there early!

QUIET AT CHRISTMAS

To be quiet at Christmas
How rare a thing!
Except for those enclosed
In shameful solitude,
Friendless and forgotten . . .
But for most of us it's
Rush and bustle,
Shopping, posting, phoning,
Eating, drinking, talking –
Glass-in-hand shouting-match parties –
Noise upon noise, to drive away
The solstice devils of darkness . . .
And in every home the essential Christmas custom:
The tattle of non-stop telly . . .

But, oh! to sit *quiet,*
To think of Christmases gone by,
Old friends, old loves, who are no more . . .
To think what Christmas *means,*
To wrap ourselves round in thought,
To be individuals again,
Not just lost in the crowd, caught up
In the jolly conglomeration
Of compulsory social Christmas,
But a man, a woman, alone,
Distinct, isolated,
A temporary speck of flesh –

Yet through this Nativity
In touch with eternity,
With wondrous, unspeakable majesty
Of vast and starry skies,
With perfect, personal love
Expressed in this new-born child . . .

To feel *this*, and in the *silence*
To let it sink in,
Is Christmas.

NATIVITY UPDATE

If Jesus Christ were born today,
Where would it be? Where would it be?
On the telly, for all to see?
Would we be shown the Infant Lord
In some brand-new maternity ward,
With neat, pretty nurses, and now and then,
White-coated Wise obstetrical Men?

If Jesus Christ were born today,
Where would it be? Where would it be?
Somewhere obscure, with few to see:
In some shabby mistal, remote in the Dales,
Amidst smelly cow-muck and swishing of tails,
With fell-weathered shepherds, privileged to peep
At the fair Lamb of God, serenely asleep.

If Jesus Christ were born today,
Where would it be? Where would it be?
Deep in the hearts of you and me!
If Jesus now into our lives we invite
'No room at the inn' is more than put right;
An updated welcome reserved just for him:
The cup of our Christmas filled up to the brim!

EPIPHANY

Three Wise Men, we say,
Three Kings . . .
Not so:
Just who they were
And how many
We shall never know:
Magi from the East
Is all Matthew says:
No rank or number,
But three memorable gifts
Justify romance
And hint a royal visitation:
Gold, for they honoured a King,
Frankincense, for they worshipped a God,
Myrrh, for they glimpsed suffering,
Even death on a Cross,
Beyond the bright Star:
Caspar, Melchior, Balthasar,
So tradition names them . . .
But nameless, unnumbered,
We treasure the tale:
For, following the Jewish shepherds,
These were the *first,*
Just like ourselves,
Gentiles who honour the Christ,
Only we far less worthy,
Our gifts to each other
Amply awarding,
And our gifts to *him* . . .
Not worth recording.

THE CHILD FROM HEAVEN

(Translation of the French carol 'Il est né le divin enfant')

Chorus

He is born, the Child from heaven,
Let the merry pipes proclaim it!
He is born, the Child from heaven,
Let us sing the Saviour's birth!

1. For more than four thousand years
    Prophets had foretold his coming,
    For more than four thousand years –
    Now at last the Lord appears!

2. Ah! How fair and full of charm,
    Perfect all his lovely graces!
    Ah! How fair and full of charm,
    Cradled safe from every harm.

3. In a cow-shed is where he lies,
    In his little bed of straw,
    In a cow-shed is where he lies,
    Humbled Lord of all the skies!

4. O Jesus, our Almighty King,
    Though you are a tiny baby,
    O Jesus, our Almighty King,
    We'll obey you in everything!

Chorus

He is born, the Child from heaven,
Let the merry pipes proclaim it!
He is born, the Child from heaven,
Let us sing the Saviour's birth!

THE FLIGHT TO EGYPT

'The Flight to Egypt,' teacher said,
'Took place when Herod, cruel king,
Tried to kill the infant Christ,
By soldiers he sent slaughtering.

'But Mary and Joseph took the child
And secretly left Bethlehem;
Their flight to Egypt went so well,
For God himself protected them.

'Now draw a picture,' teacher said,
'Which this story will explain.'
And so they did – and one little boy
Drew a lovely aeroplane.

'It's the flight to Egypt, Miss,' he said;
Four figures he drew, and quite unselfconscious,
Said, 'That's Mary and Joseph and Jesus –
And there's the Pilot, the one called Pontius.'

THE REFUGEE

God forgive us for our Christmas!
Help us, Lord, to blush for shame:
Frantic marathons of spending,
Practised in the Saviour's name!

Food for those who live in plenty,
Gifts for those who have no need;
Christ who came to feed the hungry,
Save us from our Christmas greed!

Save us from all feeble friendships,
From the yearly postal fuss:
Automatic Christmas greetings,
Sent to those who send to us!

Save us from the superficial,
Make our Christmas deep and fresh:
Show us in the simple stable
God revealed in Baby-flesh.

With the shepherds let us worship,
With the Wise Men let us see
How through proud and heartless Herod
Jesus was a refugee.

LAND-MINE CHRISTMAS

In memory of Princess Diana

What would you like for Christmas –
An artificial leg?
A nice new plastic hand, perhaps?
Useful when you beg . . .

Prosthetics – and *prevention,*
Is how our programme's styled:
No more the blast that lies in wait
To mutilate a child.

We'll build a world that's bomb-proof,
Brave Christmas amputee,
Where hands and feet are flesh and bone
And every child runs free.

LITTLE MARY

Mary and Joseph, hand in hand,
In the Christmas promised land,
Stars of school Nativity Play!
Anxious teachers watch and pray,
Doting parents fondly gaze,
Audience keen to lavish praise:
Mary, proud and thrilled to be
Centre stage of history,
Mother of Jesus, coveted role,
Played with grace and self-control,
For her years she's so mature –
Joseph isn't quite so sure,
Wonders what he's doing there,
With a towel round his hair,
Awkward in his stripy gown,
Wishing he could just sit down;
Like the Joseph long ago,
So much that he doesn't know,
Out, embarrassed, on a limb:
What's this got to do with him?
He's no father, that's quite clear;
Things are not what they appear . . .
Still, theology can wait,
First he must accommodate
This uniquely pregnant lass;
Carpenter with not much brass,
Can't afford to bribe a room,
In a stable, in the gloom,
Brilliant birth – which no one shows,
Though, in these days, anything goes:
Here's the baby – Oh, how sweet!
Joseph thinks: a plastic cheat,
Never cries – and, what's so strange,
Nappies they will never change!
More realistic than the birth
Shepherds bring us down to earth,

Though all seated on the ground,
Some are restless, look around,
More intent on having a peep
At Mum and Dad, than watching sheep;
Angelic message – Oh, how blessed!
The shepherds don't seem too impressed;
Glorious tidings the heavens disclose –
And a lad at the back is picking his nose!
Self-important Kings appear,
'I'm a King!' you almost hear,
Royally dressed and very keen –
And haven't they slipped in a queen?
Wicked Herod, rough loud voice –
Casting him, they're spoilt for choice!

Then to Bethlehem they go
Gathering round in grand tableau,
Pilgrims, as we all should be,
To the Christmas Mystery:
Some will say, 'It's just a show,
Kids don't understand, you know;
Croaky carols all off-key . . .'
But here's a lesson for you and me:
Wrapped in myth and fancy dress
A clue to perfect happiness:
'Through the children,' Jesus said,
'You will to the truth be led,'
Then in their midst he set a child;
And I think he would have smiled
To see himself in modern days,
In one of these Nativity Plays,
Surrounded by these childhood charms,
Safe in little Mary's arms.

CHRISTMAS CUSTOMS

Martin Luther, so they say,
Placed a candle on a tree
To bring to mind the bright new star
That shone on Christ's Nativity . . .
Then, later, Albert, German prince,
To please Victoria, wife and queen,
Set up a candled Christmas tree –
The first most English folk had seen;
And his good mate, Sir Henry Cole,
To greet his many absent friends,
Invented the first Christmas card,
While Dickens boosted Yule-tide trends
With Pickwick, Scrooge and Tiny Tim,
With goose and turkey, punch and rum,
With brandy-flaming Christmas pud
And finger-burnt Snapdragon plum!
Then Tom Smith, selling parcelled sweets,
One night sat by a great log fire:
The sparks flew up and crackled loud,
And Christmas crackers did inspire . . .
Then, choicest of Victorian fun,
The parents' secret worthy cause:
They fairy-taled Saint Nicholas,
And turned him into Santa Claus . . .
Christmas customs! Rare romance!
You colour winter's dreary face –
And yet Saint Francis bids you yield
And give to Christ the central place:
He custom-built his Christmas crib,
Where Shepherds, Wise Men, gently tread,
And hold their breath, and dare to peep
At God within a manger-bed.

TWELFTH NIGHT

From the partridge in the pear-tree
To the twelve drummers drumming,
It's all over now:
Down with the decorations,
Prickling the fingers
On holly and spruce tree;
Pack up the baubles,
Collect all the cards,
Then away with the manger . . .

How bare the rooms look!
How boring our food seems,
With lingering remnants
Of dreary cold turkey!

For a while we have lived
Like millionaires,
Like Lords a-leaping,
Cocooned from the winter,
Immune from all time:

Now, down to earth,
But not with a bump:
Gently, thankfully,
Peace in our hearts,
Our spirits refreshed,
Facing the future,
Knowing that whatever will fill
The diary's blank pages
The cheerful chaos of Christmas,
As certain as death,
Will lighten our darkness once again.

NOTES ON CHRISTMAS ORIGINS

p.5   Both Matthew (2:1) and Luke (1:5) set the birth of Jesus in the reign of Herod the Great (d. 4 BC). Because of later confusion in the calendar scholars believe Jesus could have been born as early as 6 BC.

p.6   Christingle services originated with the eighteenth century Moravians. Children carry a lighted candle stuck in a decorated orange, with the symbolism as given in the poem.

p.11   ' . . . when he shall come again in his glorious majesty to judge the quick and the dead' (Collect for Advent).

p.9   'And the Word was made flesh and dwelt among us' (John 1:14).

p.13   The first known Christmas card was designed for (Sir) Henry Cole (a friend of Prince Albert) by J. C. Horsley in 1843. Four years later Queen Victoria sent fifty-six Christmas cards. Now a thousand million are sent in the UK alone.

p.15   25th December was the high point of the Roman festival of Saturnalia, held to mark the winter solstice. Its adoption by Christians to celebrate the birth of Christ is first mentioned in 336 AD.

p.20   The Incarnation (from Latin *carnis,* flesh) is the doctrine that God became man in Christ (John 1:14-18).

p.21   G. A. Studdert-Kennedy was a well-respected chaplain in the First World War, nicknamed by the soldiers 'Woodbine Willie'.

p.24   Jesus was a refugee, along with Mary and Joseph (Matthew 2:13-15).

p.25   Charles Dickens had an infectious enthusiasm for Christmas, seen especially in *A Christmas Carol* (1843), with its vivid portrayal of Ebenezer Scrooge.

p.27   Bing Crosby's version of Irving Berlin's song (1941) is the best-selling gramophone record of all time.

p.33   UNICEF estimates that twelve million children a year die of malnutrition and preventable disease.

p.34   See also the instruction given to Joseph (Matthew 1:21).

p.44   The racial prejudice which might well have been typical of Roman soldiers is here tempered by tenderness.

p.45   Emmanuel is Hebrew for 'God with us' (Matthew 1:23).

p.46   St Nicholas was the fourth-century Bishop of Myra, noted for generous, anonymous giving, as in this legend. The Dutch version of his name used by settlers in America, *Sinter Klaas*, gave us 'Santa Claus'.

p.50   This poem was read one Christmas morning on the radio by the late Wilfred Pickles.

p.59   The Devil's Knell is tolled at All Saints, Dewsbury, Yorkshire, ending at midnight on Christmas Eve. The bell, Black Tom, is said to have been presented in the fifteenth century by Thomas Soothill, by as a penance after he had murdered a servant.

p.62   By an Act of Parliament in 1652 it was decreed that 'no observation shall be had of the Five and Twentieth day of December, commonly called Christmas Day'. Though the Act was never repealed, the festival was observed with traditional vigour following the Restoration of Charles II in 1660.

p.64   This was a prize-winning poem in a competition organised by the *Times Educational Supplement* (1987) for a modern version of Milton's 'Ode on the Morning of Christ's Nativity'.

p.66   The first turkeys are believed to have been brought to England in the sixteenth century by William Strickland, who had sailed with Sebastian Cabot to the Americas. They were landed near Bridlington ('Bollinton') and bred on the Strickland estate at Boynton.

p.77   John Wesley (1703-91) said on his deathbed, 'The best of all is, God is with us.' Describing his conversion in 1738 he had said, 'My heart was strangely warmed.'

p.80   The Jehovah's Witnesses, like the Puritans of 1652, do not celebrate Christmas.

p.90   The first royal Christmas radio broadcast was made by George V in 1932.

p.94   Mistletoe was venerated by the Celts whose priests, the Druids, cut it with a golden sickle at the winter solstice. Tablets containing an extract from the berries have been prescribed to lower hypertension.

p.97   Epiphany commemorates the visit of the Wise Men or Magi, as described in Matthew's Gospel. He does not say that they were kings or that there were three of them, but this has been assumed from the mention of three gifts. He also implies that the visit took place when Jesus was no longer a new-born baby (Matthew 2:1-16). Epiphany is observed on 6th January.

p.98   This is a new translation of a carol which the author taught to schoolchildren over many years in the original French.

p.99   Matthew 2:13-15.

p.104   Christmas trees became popular in England after Prince Albert set one up for Queen Victoria and their children at Windsor in 1841. By 1848 the royal custom was featured in the *Illustrated London News*. Tom Smith got his idea for Christmas crackers in about 1860. St Francis of Assisi made the first known Nativity scene, using full-size wooden figures and real animals, at Greccio, northern Italy, in 1223.

INDEX